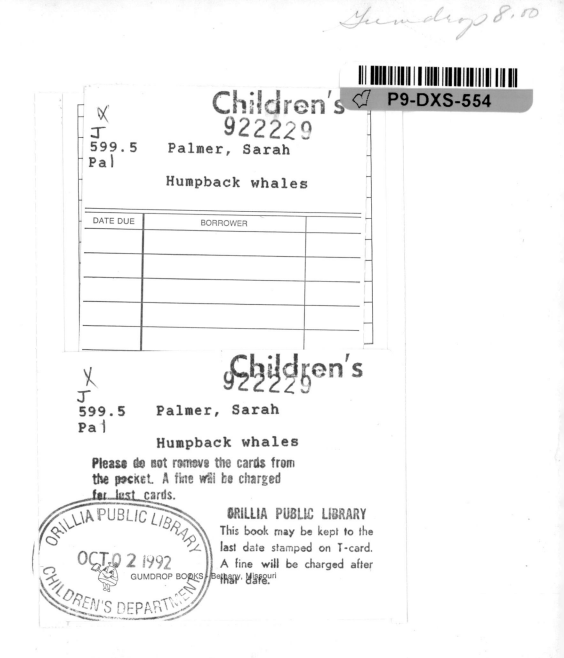

Children's
922229

X
J
599.5
Pal

Palmer, Sarah

Humpback whales

DATE DUE	BORROWER	

Children's
922229

X
J
599.5
Pal

Palmer, Sarah

Humpback whales

Please do not remove the cards from
the pocket. A fine will be charged
for lost cards.

ORILLIA PUBLIC LIBRARY
This book may be kept to the
last date stamped on T-card.
A fine will be charged after
that date.

HUMPBACK WHALES

THE WHALE DISCOVERY LIBRARY

Sarah Palmer

Illustrated by Tony Gibbon

Rourke Enterprises, Inc.
Vero Beach, Florida 32964

Library of Congress Cataloging-in-Publication Data

Palmer, Sarah, 1955-
  Humpback Whales.

922220

  (The Whale discovery library)
  Includes index.
  Summary: Describes the physical appearance, habits,
diet, and habitat of the humpback whale and threats to
its existence.
  1. Humpback Whale—Juvenile literature. [1. Humpback
Whale. 2. Whales] I. Title. II. Series:
Palmer, Sarah, 1955-
Whale discovery library.
QL737.C424P35 1989   599.5'1   88-3238
ISBN 0-86592-478-3

TABLE OF CONTENTS

HUMPBACK WHALES

Humpback whales are often seen leaping from the water. This is called **breaching**. They look happy, but humpbacks are always itchy. They suffer from **parasites** that live on their skin and tickle them. When the humpback whales breach, they slap themselves hard down on the water. It looks as if they are trying to shake the parasites off their skin.

Humpback whales are often seen breaching

HOW THEY LOOK

Humpback whales have the longest flippers of any whale. Their flippers are about 14 feet long and have a bumpy front edge. The skin of the humpback whales is dark along their back. They are white underneath and under their long flippers. Humpback whales can grow up to 60 feet long. An average humpback weighs over 40 tons.

Humpback whales have very long, bumpy flippers

WHERE THEY LIVE

Humpback whales live in the North Atlantic and North Pacific Oceans. Humpbacks **migrate** to warmer waters in the cold winter months. It takes them three months to reach their new homes in Bermuda or the Hawaiian Islands. Humpbacks always migrate to exactly the same place each year. They defend their right to that **territory**. Humpback whales are often seen close to shore.

9

Humpback whales often swim close to shore

WHAT THEY EAT

Humpback whales eat small fish and tiny plants called **plankton**. This food is strained through the whale bones in their cheeks. These bones are called **baleen plates**. Humpback whales herd schools of fish into a tight group. This way they can get many fish into their mouths in one try. Sometimes seabirds peck at the schools of fish the whales have rounded up. If they are not careful, they also get swallowed by the humpbacks!

Humpback whales feed on tiny fish and plants

Humpback whales suffer from
skin parasites

The songs of the humpback whales are very beautiful

LIVING IN THE OCEAN

Whales talk to each other underwater. They use a series of clicks and whistles. These noises are also used to help the whales find their way. The echoes from the sounds the whales make are bounced off objects in the water. The whale can tell from the echo what the objects are. Sometimes the sounds whales make are like singing. The beautiful ''songs'' of the humpback whales are very famous.

Humpback whales can "talk"
each other underwater

BABY HUMPBACK WHALES

Newborn humpback whales, called **calves**, do not have any **blubber**. Blubber is the thick layer of fat under the whales' skin. It keeps the whales warm in the freezing oceans. Humpback calves would not survive if they were born in the cold northern seas. They are born after the family has migrated to warmer waters for the winter. The baby humpback is a darker color than its parents.

Baby humpbacks are darker gray than their parents

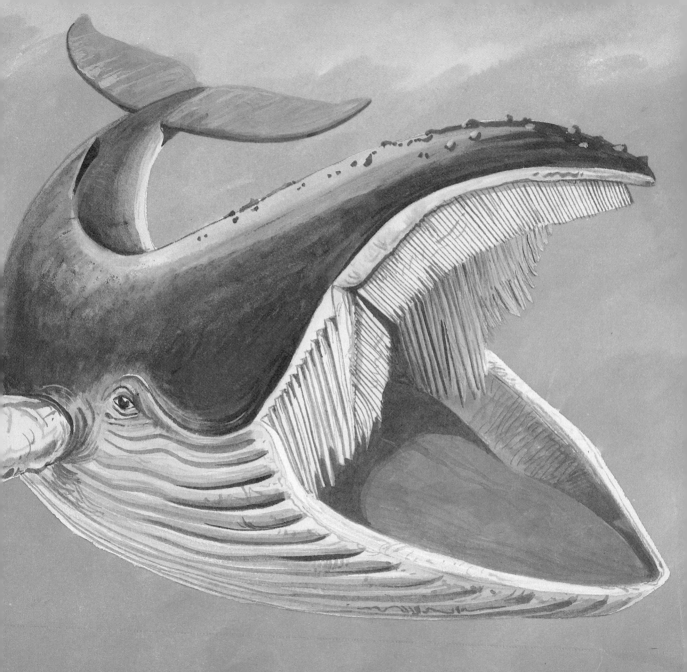

HUMPBACK WHALES AND PEOPLE

Humpback whales were hunted for their baleen plates or whale bone. These plates are very strong and quite **flexible**. Whale bone was used for fashionable ladies' corsets. The bristles on the baleen plates also had many uses. They were used for making wigs and for stuffing furniture. The blubber of humpback whales was used for making oil.

Humpback whales were hunted for their baleen plates

SAVING HUMPBACK WHALES

Humpback whales are slow swimmers. They like to swim close to shore. This made humpbacks easy **prey** for the **whalers**. In the early part of this century there were very few humpback whales left in the oceans. The whalers had killed nearly all of them. No one is allowed to kill humpback whales anymore. Scientists believe there are about 10,000 humpbacks left in the world.

Humpback whales were easy prey for the whalers

FACT FILE

Common Name: Humpback Whale
Scientific Name: Megaptera novaeangliae
Type: Baleen whale
Color: Gray
Size: up to 60 feet
Weight: up to 40 tons
Number in World: 10,000

Glossary

baleen plates (BAL een PLATES) — whalebones used to strain food in a whale's mouth

blubber (BLUB ber) — a thick layer of fat under a whale's skin

to breach (BREACH) — to leap clear of the water

calves (CALVES) — young whales

flexible (FLEX i ble) — able to be bent

to migrate (MI grate) — to move from one place to another, usually at the same time each year

parasites (PAR a sites) — animals that depend on others for food without giving anything in return

plankton (PLANK ton) — tiny plants on which whales feed

prey (PREY) — an animal hunted by another for food

territory (TER ri tor y) — a claimed area of land or sea

whalers (WHAL ers) — people who hunt whales

23

INDEX